Cowgirls

Sherri London Pastolove

Cowgirls

Copyright @ 2018 by Sherri London Pastolove

All rights reserved.

ISBN 13: 978-0692091517
ISBN 10: 0692091513
Library of Congress Control Number: 2018903322
Sherri London Pastolove
Westbury, NY

for Sharyn, Harriet and Nicole…

and all the cowgirls

Contents

Cowgirls	1
July 1967	2
19th Amendment	3
Lake Carmel Memories	4
Pink Moon	5
Where Summer Seeps In	6
Golden	7
After the Fall	8
Blood Red	9
Open Road	10
Bewitched Bothered and Bewildered	11
Valentine's Day	12
Comfort	13
Writer's Lament	14
Song of Solomon	15
Waiting to Exhale	16
The Wild Blue	17
Joe's	18
Word Swept	20
Common Scents	21
Illumination	22
Trains	23
The Gold Rush	24
Home	26
On Drowning	28
Scars	29
Unspoken	30
Rain	31
Water	32
Niagara Falls	33

Kaddish	34
Yom HaShoah	35
Benediction	36
In Memoriam	37
Tremors (for Sharyn)	38
Sea Glass	39
Gravitas	40
Revelation	41
Redemption Song	42
La Vérité	43
Acknowledgements	45
About the Author	47

Cowgirls

I woke up with Waylon Jennings in my head
crooning with Willie Nelson
about babies and cowboys,
and wondered about the
fate of cowgirls,
defiant braids escaping their hats,
horseback in the blazing sun
hurtling for the horizon

but the roar of the shower
and whine of the coffee maker
pushed this aside;
there is comfort in the chatter
of my daily grind

it drowns all memory
of hurt revealed
in the halting conversation
of today's cowgirls,
a generation
hiding its longing
behind the safety
of a firewall

I look for my lasso
to reign them in,
these cowgirls,
and hold them tight

there is no warmth
in a waning campfire

July 1967

I want you to braid my hair

don't comb an even part -
let me feel the warmth
of your fingertips
gently tickling my scalp
as you silently count
one...two…three…

firmly grasp my hair
as you tame
all that is wild
into neat plaits,
then sigh at success
as a brightly colored
rubber band is snapped
into place at the end

yes, braid my hair
even though
a defiant curl will
escape at my brow
in this summer heat,
to let you know
it is me

19th Amendment

I liked the old voting booths,
the memory of crowding in
with my brother and mom,
looking up at her in earnestness,
making faces at my brother
all the while inhaling the
mustiness of cheap worn curtains,
for a brief moment we were
with the wizard,
choosing the fate of two men,
and our country as it were

but all I wanted was to pull
that heavy lever and listen
to the snap of metal and fabric,
then land back in the school gym
amazed at the sight
of so many moms around us,
hair teased to the heavens,
fingers tightly holding
those of my friends,
a serious air wafting
above the booths
sailing through worn windowpanes
into the Brooklyn streets

then that evening,
huddled around the
black and white screen,
Walter Cronkite reading results
deep into the night,
his voice reassuring a
tired nation,
his proclamation sealing
our fate.

Lake Carmel Memories

it is summertime
and I am at Lake Carmel for
my annual stay at my aunt and uncle's house
and I am in heaven
I get to spend an entire week
with my beloved cousin, Jennifer,
three and a half years my senior;
she is more like a big sister
and I, the devoted younger sister

we will wear our matching bathing suits
and float on the worn rafts at the lake
toasting in the sun
my pale skin freckling,
her deep olive skin almost chocolate

we will sing along to the songs
drifting from the transistor radios along the shore
we will laugh as my aunt chases
the Good Humor truck as we depart,
honking her horn for him to stop
and we'll eat our ice cream
in the car, before dinner,
vanilla dribbling down our necks

on the drive back to the house
my aunt will stop at the little convenience store
and treat us to cut outs, which will
keep us amused for hours into the night
I will carefully take my favorite book
from my aunt's bookshelf,
the childhood poetry collection,
"The Owl and the Pussycat" over and over
my uncle smiling, taking mental notes
he will be the first to buy me a poetry book,
which I still have buried deep in my bookshelf

Pink Moon

I heard there would be a
pink moon on my
birthday this year,
and so I waited for sunset and
searched the April sky,
but all that I saw was a
plain white moon,
as sad and lonely as
a glass of milk without cookies

and I looked again with longing
and imagined the moon
veiled in hues of pink,
the blush of newborn cheeks
and sticky cotton candy
lipstick of toddlers,
the frosty noses
of youthful snowball fights
and the flushed ear tips
of a first crush,
an iced satin prom gown,
a bouquet bursting
with soft rose petals on
thorny stems,
petals that you pressed
and saved in a book
on the shelf
to savor and hold in your hand
on a dark cold moonless night,
reminding you of the
promise of a pink April moon

Where Summer Seeps In

in the small space
where you left the window open
the rain came in,
a sweeping spray
now beads of water
on the windowsill
as the cat sits
tormenting them
like prey

nearby sounds slip through,
the roar of the
neighbor's dog
becomes a muffled whimper,
joyous cries for the
ice cream truck
are whispers,
and the truck's song
a memory

I can smell
the fading glory of lilacs,
a hint of roses
about to bloom,
and the musty scent of
summer rain
finding its way
in the small space
where you left the window open,
these gifts you left me
on a lazy afternoon

Golden

Neil Young is down
by the river,
and I'm driving north
dirty traffic soon
a blur in the rear view,
fall color bursts approaching
in burnt orange
and crimson-flecked gold
highway exits sparse,
mountains reach higher,
en pointe, towards the heavens,
coaxing me,
whispering softly…
"we are stardust, we are golden"
Joni Mitchell on high

After the Fall

After the fall,
when leaves are nothing more
than crisp remnants underfoot,
and the landscape wide and barren

after the fall,
when the wicker bowl that
held the fragrant bounty of your garden,
sits empty and forlorn, yearning for spring

after the fall,
when your hands that once
cupped the ocean's might in joy,
now twist and ache in woolen wrappings

and after the fall,
when you look to the sun,
a lonely ray to warm your soul,
leave your booted footprints
behind on a winter white afternoon

Blood Red

the blade,
smooth as ocean stone,
glistens in a lone sunray,
my warped reflection
blankly staring back

the handle,
a weight in my hand,
heavy with impatience
as iridescent pearls
of sweat dot my palm

the tip,
sharp and piercing,
like icy January mornings
that turn breath to frost,
grasping withered grass
in despair

I raise the knife and
split the apple with disregard,
the seeds scattering
like worker ants on the march
beyond the cutting board's edge,
the slices, motionless, waiting
as I grab them one by one,
devouring their sweetness
on a bitter winter afternoon

Open Road

Ambling along harbor road,
the trees now bend and twist
trying to hide
their new nakedness,
autumn's glory a fading memory

the sky looms large this morning
a solemn pastiche of grey and muddy blue,
cold winds toss
leaves into the air,
those green bag runaways,
their fate unknown

boats huddle in the harbor,
masts wrapped tight,
they dream of July
and her dazzling sun,
beckoning them to
open seas

but me,
I'm turning up
the radio,
singing loud with Tom Petty
as we drive into the
great wide open,
a twinkle in my eye,
winter's abyss chasing
exhaust plumes in vain

Bewitched Bothered and Bewildered

Because the cat
knocked the plant
from the stand,
soil and leaves
splattered on the
just vacuumed
carpet,

and

because the
dryer exhaled
its last breath,
our clothes hung
like tinsel
throughout
the apartment

and

because I left
the bags of
groceries in the trunk,
for hours
on this
hot summer day,

meet me on the
fire escape,
we'll dine on
Ritz crackers
as we sip
red wine served
in styrofoam cups,
laughing under a
bewitching summer
moon

Valentine's Day

Don't sing me love songs,
someone else's
light heart
  full heart
    broken heart

Or send flowers
that will smile,
then bend,
and soon lay in defeat,
scattered on my
piano

Don't bring me chocolates,
the lush
or bittersweet,
a momentary rush
and then
sadness in an empty
cardboard box

No,
on Valentine's Day
just smile,
your hand in mine,
like Cupid's arrow,
its heat
piercing a cold
winter's day

Comfort

He didn't like floral comforters,
wanted to drift to sleep
wrapped in
monochromatic cotton;
she liked roses floating
in fields of rich
jewel-toned sateen -
Dorothy running
through a sea
of poppies

this, the
thread of debate,
huddled under the
worn blanket of those first years,
until détente

and now,
the weight of
age and life
renders quick sleep
under their
Ralph Lauren flowers,
bookends,
cocooned till dawn

Writer's Lament

If I could write,
I would write you
a chocolate cake,
and frost it with
carefully chosen phrases,
not sugar-laden
clichés from the can

or if I could write,
I would write you
a late summer day,
burnt-orange sky,
cicadas singing in your ear,
not the grating bark
of our neighbor's dog

but today I cannot write,
and so it is
peanut butter and jelly,
as we listen
to August rain
drip into the
bucket by the door

Song of Solomon

Fingers entwined, I see
my hands, summer-browned
skin growing translucent
in the light

you hold them close
and I remember
the unblemished
glow of our youth
when you sang me
your Song of Solomon
as I danced under
the Mexican moonlight
my toes burning in the sand

oh, how I never took care
to wrap my feet in cool cloths
nor bathed them in ancient myrrh
to preserve their strength for
our long journey across
oceans and deserts,
rocks and dirt,
busy roads and desolate
winding paths that
disappeared among the
clouds that now float
in a teacup that you
gently place in my hands
as darkness wraps us
on a late summer night

Waiting to Exhale

She said,
"where'd you buy
that smile?"
as I drove off
with a wave,
grinning from
brow to
toe

I swore
over that second
cup of coffee
not to utter a word,
afraid I would
exhale my happiness
into the cool
morning air

my breath sharp
like a pin,
piercing my yellow
balloon,
sending it
ricocheting
to earth

the corners of
my mouth
spiraling
downward

as you walked away

The Wild Blue

Fingers firmly grasp the rail
droplets of salty sea water
speckle her skirt
eyes search the endless
ocean, indigo,
on a sunless day

deep breaths,
the cool brine
quickens her pulse,
the feverish fetid days
in steerage forgotten,
like the silent sadness
of memory

chestnut locks riding
the breeze,
lips of crushed
rose petals
pursed in thought,
she turns
to meet his gaze

flickers of fire
in her wild blue eyes
melt his stoic heart,
the future sailing
onward in the corners of
a smile

Joe's

Squinting at me with
whiskeyed eyes,
Bob opens his mouth,
cigarette stained teeth
flickering in desperation,
but then retreat,
as he reaches for his glass
and disappears

Joe's on Tuesday nights

Willie,
beer soaked remnants
of his paycheck,
the ante tossed on the table
as the crowd claps,
he aims for glory,
a withered dartboard
laughs in reply

Trish,
sneaking to the ladies'
to count her tips,
and rest her feet
at odds tonight with worn heels,
the black satins that
caressed sheer silk hose
on long shuttered dance floors
dotting Route 29

Joe,
smiling from a yellowed photograph
in a lopsided frame
buried behind the cheap scotch bottles,
a burly mustached man,
arms tightly wrapped around
two pretty red lipped blondes,
beer in hand

and me, gently brushing raindrops
from my hair,
while drinking memories
out of chipped shot glasses,
at Joe's on a Tuesday night

Word Swept

my umbrella snaps in defeat,
no match for this downpour

words rain down,
the used and discarded of
poets who came before me,
breathing other lives,
exhaling the wistful
plumes of dreamers

slivers of syntax shimmering
in a warm October mist.

Common Scents

I hate the smell of Penn Station

from arrival in its deep bowels
on dank platforms
drenched in the scent of greasy food
and the perfume of
aching, ancient machinery
longing for the scrap yard

then climbing the stairs
a fetid feast underfoot
lacquered coffee streams
paper-bagged beer gone astray
gum, long robbed of its minty joy
and other liquids I choose to ignore

oh, and all that humanity packed
in walkways and corridors and exits
the assault of incongruous aromas
freshly bathed, never bathed
leave me gasping, and rushing
with determination
as the desperation of a rotting city
burns my nostrils

escalators carry me above
I pause to breathe,
my disgust and sadness
exhaled in odorless plumes
that soar and vanish
above steely skyscrapers
in an ashen morning sky

Illumination

In the supermarket,
clutching a yahrzeit candle
that I will light this evening
a small glass
white wax and sadness
but I smile
recalling the strange
juxtaposition of those
glasses in my youth
ablaze in my grandmother's kitchen
only to resurface days later
as vessels for milk
served with freshly baked
cookies stored in
aluminum lined shoe boxes
everything to be used again
the vestiges of impoverished youth
in shtetls far away
so foreign to generations
twice removed
wrapped in the
warmth of our casual excess

I hold the memory
of the raconteurs,
my beloved grandmother
and her dear sisters,
deep within me,
tears flowing
as I strike the match
and pray

Trains

There were always trains
on New Year's Eve
graffiti splattered subways awash
in the stale smell of inebriated revelers
and youthful desperation

and later, commuter cars
that carried me
away from the belly of the city
that fed my soul,
and left me thirsty in the
solitude of pristine suburbia

I think of that now,
cashmere, rouged smile
at midnight,
my lifetime suspended in the
effervescent bubbles of a champagne flute
as memory crests the surface
in little bursts -

tequila stained Levi's,
nameless faces,
so many broken resolutions
worn and fragile
like a stray yellowed photograph
buried deep beneath
woolen socks and ripped stockings,
in the back of that old dresser

mascara laden eyes smiling back
at a long-forgotten photographer,
my face sandwiched
between the masses
on a downtown 1 train
as midnight nipped my heels
on New Year's Eve

The Gold Rush

It is August
it is always August

we sit in the back seat
imaginary dividing line
my side, your side

a sideways glance
a grin, unspoken
declaration of war
the line is crossed,
we giggle and wrestle,
dad's voice thunders
from behind the wheel,
we retreat

hours and miles on 95 South
the heat presses through
air-conditioned windows,
lulling us to sleep

the ocean waves of
Daytona break at our
feet, sweep our sandcastles
out to the Atlantic,
sun kissed skin
and late night ice cream cones,
days of heaven

August
your move out west
just weeks away -
the twenty-first century gold rush
as we all jump the waves

they say Lebanon, Kansas
is the center of the U.S. –
be sure to cross it
in the back of that old car,
dad's voice whispering
in the sky

Home

The house that
spoke in creaks
and rattles,
leaving me
tossing and
turning all night.

and then
the house that
softly hummed
a lullaby,
rocking me
into a deep slumber.

old walls that
echoed with
toddler tears,
midnight meows,
lunchtime laughter,
swelling with the joy
of family festivities.

windows facing
lush greens, or
mounds of snow,
and always trees.
the birch –
laced with white,
the cherry blossom -
its promise of pink,
and the maple -
vibrant orange in the fall.

I will pack lightly,
bottle the memories,
and pour them
into the corners
wherever I go,
close my eyes,
inhale the sweetness
of home

On drowning

I try to swim
tread water
memory cupped
in my hands
a red team jacket
chlorine burning my throat
legs numb
one hundred laps
stroke
        stroke
                breathe

but I am drowning
sinking under the
weight of my own
expectation

a scribbled list
of wants and needs
floats beyond
my grasp
leaves me
spiraling
naked to the core

the next wave
roars in the distance
I summon the strength
inhale
        stretch
                gasp

and silence
as I break the surface

Scars

Ever touch a scar
then lose yourself in
the wonderment of
every cell
every heartbeat
the power of blood
coursing through your veins
your lungs rising and falling
in perfect syncopation

when poised under
the harsh surgical lamps,
cold grey enveloping you,
the scalpel lowered
as you were opened,
lay bare,
what was lost?

a memory,
a secret hope
floating beyond
the surgeon's grasp
caught in twisted skin,
a scar that your fingertips
trace in longing

your lungs wait in
chevron formation
open your eyes
breathe deep
as dawn creeps
through the curtain seams
on a Tuesday morning

Unspoken

It was in the way your
shoulders slumped
ever so slightly
barely noticeable
that I saw
how that umbilical cord,
never really cut,
remained an invisible
bridge that tethers
you to me

your countenance,
the stoicism of
newly-minted adulthood,
I was the one mute tear
that caressed
your cheek,
floodgates of anguish
in check

in the morning grey
my lips move in silence
as I pray
for rain to wash
off the dirt of this
world

Rain

I'm gonna sit
on that old
bench in the rain.

no umbrella
or raincoat -

gonna let
those raindrops roll
down my cheeks,
slip into the space
at the nape of my neck,
dampen my hair
till it turns
chestnut

catch the cool
late afternoon storm
in the palms of
my hands,
socks soaked
as puddles slip
through sneaker seams

I'm just gonna
sit there,
smile through
windswept showers,
watch that spring sky
cry tears of joy,
blessing
me before
night falls

Water

Again the earth shakes,
and then, the water

Always the water

A tsunami ravaging
all memory,
youth with only
textbook tales,
second-hand stories,
whisper
new narratives of numbness

Always the water

They cry of thirst
in regions ruled
by despots
disease
drought

They run,
then vanish
in twisted
tenacious
typhoons

And sometimes
you can still
hear the water
in nervous laughter
on Bourbon Street

Images of eyes
awash in tears
flood humanity,
pull us to the vortex,
as we
swim towards salvation.

Always the water

Niagara Falls

When the day came crashing
down,
cascading, then thrashing
in its fury,
and I, like the rocks,
back turned in
ignorant bliss,
never knowing
as my face turned to
meet the sun's
fading smile,
how I would
be swallowed
whole,
swept out
like the
age-worn rocks,
slate, and even like
discarded souvenirs,
drowned deep
in memory

Kaddish

I say Kaddish
to myself,
a rote response,
a quiet plea

My faith is crushed
in the avalanche of
photos of children,
flowers plucked
before blooming

My heart in pieces
under the weight of
the tears of mothers,
and fathers,
and in that
catch in the
throats of
seasoned reporters

I say Kaddish again
praying that if I
don't hear the answer,
that I will be blessed,
and forget
the question

Yom HaShoah

A generation gently
fades from this earth,
survivors, warriors,
the memory keepers,
now buried
beneath Stars of David,
Kaddish whispered on cliffs,
as ashes cascade
into the ocean's abyss

and the millions -
reduced to a paragraph
in history books never read

the assertions, eyes smiling,
"it is a myth,
this Holocaust you speak of"
there are no number-branded
arms left to reply

I light the candle,
this mitzvah of remembrance,
and see thousands of souls
dancing in its illumination,
praying for new warriors
yet to be born

Benediction

I'll call you eggshell blue,
this September sky
swollen with our loss,
the souls of those we
loved, of those we
never knew
but cried for as
summer slipped
into golden autumn that year
today I will not watch
those children who are
children no more
I will not listen to
the bells ring against
a skyline I do not
recognize
today I will
walk in silence
and toss coins
into imaginary fountains,
passage for the lost souls
to cross endless rivers of memory
on this eggshell blue
Monday morning

In Memoriam

Perhaps it is as it
should be,
an endless line of
humanity weaving
through a roped
entrance,
complacently
adhering to
security checks,
and then
finally
arriving in
a place of
deafening solitude

From the pools
where the towers,
North and South,
once stood tall,
the windswept splay of water
is welcomed,
the cool mist
washing away
the silent tears

hands reach for
endless names
carved for posterity,
the soft prayers,
to many gods,
in many languages
echo one voice
broken in
eternal sorrow

Tremors
(for Sharyn)

This is how an earthquake starts

you wake up,
blissfully unaware of the
seismic shift of earth
that rolled underfoot,
while you skipped stones
across crystal clear ponds
under a blue July sky
in that 3am dream,
the lush green fields of summer
pulled you in deeper,
as the earth fractured,
leaving hairline cracks
down to the core of
all you knew,
   all you loved,
      all you were.

Sea Glass

Beyond the weathered rocks
and shattered shells,
the tangle of twisted seaweed
and sting of white-crested waves,
alone in the silence of indigo blue,
I cry your name

it roars along the
ocean floor
and washes up,
a whisper buried
in sea glass,
translucent green,
that now dangles from
weathered brown lace
around my neck,
a remembrance of
salty giggles,
our summer lullaby
soaring high above
the endless indigo blue

Gravitas

Summer lacks gravitas

it is not in the gait of
long legs lightly
touching the sand at dusk,
nor in the bend of elbows
shucking sweet corn
on hot mornings

it is not in the tinkling
of ice cubes splashing
in pastel plastic cups
at Sunday barbecues,
nor is it in the pause as
you hold your breath
while diving in the deep end
just one more time

there is no gravitas in summer
just the muted sorrow of
tears melting behind that
old pair of Ray Bans you
bought in the warmth of youth,
never thinking of the chill
in a late August morning

Revelation

Revelation 3:16
"So then because thou art lukewarm, and neither cold nor hot, I will spue thee out of my mouth"

A passage from a bible I do not claim as mine,
rests with me days after first hearing it

Its meanings sweetening my subconscious
like the last piece of chocolate
savored all alone

How many choose the lukewarm,
drifting safely, babe in the bathwater,
decade to decade,
floating to sea,
not even a footprint in the sand?

We flinch as genius tempts the flame,
and hardly mask our envy
as the detached coolly
collect candles for the cake

But neither sinner,
nor saint
we seek grace and mercy in
our despair,
yet leave the gift of life
on the table,
still wrapped in
ribbons of gold

Redemption Song

I heard the church bells
while crossing main street,
their faraway song,
a plea for hope
reverberating through
a bitter January sky

and I was cold
my coat threadbare,
wool scarf flapping in surrender
as the wind bit my face

iced to my core
those bells taunted me,
a dare from the heavens
to look up in joy
not downward in contempt

I plodded onward as the first flakes fell,
took refuge in the corner coffee shop
looking for salvation in a fresh brew,
and found redemption in the tepid 11 am
smile from the weary waitress,
blessed Mary, full of grace

La Vérité

I don't want to be

liberalized, conservatized
nationalized, socialized
baptized, evangelized
demonized, radicalized
homogenized, fractionalized
polarized, galvanized
jeopardized, ostracized
womanized, marginalized
antagonized, victimized
terrorized, institutionalized
unrecognized

I
just
want
to
be

Acknowledgements

The author is grateful to the editors of the following publications, where some of these poems first appeared:

Long Island Pulse Magazine – "Niagara Falls", "Water", "Word Swept", "Writer's Lament"
Nassau County Poet Laureate Society Review Vol II – "Golden"
Nassau County Poet Laureate Society Review Vol III – "Cowgirls"
Nassau County Poet Laureate Society Review Vol IV – "Sea Glass"
Nassau County Poet Laureate Society Review Vol V – "Illumination"
Newsday – "Valentine's Day"
911 Memorial Artists Registry – "In Memoriam"

About the Author

Sherri London Pastolove was born in Brooklyn, NY and received her BFA from NYU's Tisch School of the Arts. Her first poetry collection, *Love in D Major* (iUniverse, 2010), explored the many facets of life, both ordinary and extraordinary. Those reflections go somewhat deeper in this new collection, *Cowgirls*, as life experience often does as we move forward. Her work has appeared in *Newsday*, *Long Island Pulse Magazine*, and several editions of *The Nassau County Poet Laureate Society Review*. As a New York writer, she is proudest of her inclusion in the *911 Memorial Artist Registry*.

When not agonizing over her latest poem, Sherri can be found blogging at "What Do You Say, Sherri Darling" @ www.sherridarling.blogspot.com

www.ingramcontent.com/pod-product-compliance
Lightning Source LLC
LaVergne TN
LVHW021625080426
835510LV00019B/2765